Long live Impressionism

& Pointillism!

from Monet to Matisse

Catherine de Duve

KATE'ART EDITIONS

POINT

A few years later it is in the café Montesquieu at thc Palais Royal that the "independents" meet up. They are the new or **Neo impressionists,** also called **divisionists** and **pointillists,** because they divide colours and apply them point by point following a scientific principle. From close up, pure colours are jotted down next to one another; yet they appear blended from a distance. Our eyes' retina does the work. It is an optical effect! But who are these new painters and those influenced by them?

Seurat
1859-1891

Signac
1863-1935

Cross
1856-1910

Luce
1858-1941

Lemmen
1865-1916

Van Gogh
1853-1890

A NAKED WOMAN!

Who is this beauty posing on enveloping cushions? It is Olympia, a *courtisan,* and she is staring at us. One of her mules just slipped on her embroidered shawl. Whilst her maid is presenting her with the flower bouquet of an admirer, Olympia only looks at us and we can't take our eyes away from her. Ksssh… A small black cat arches its back and turns his round inquisitive eyes towards us. Can you see him?

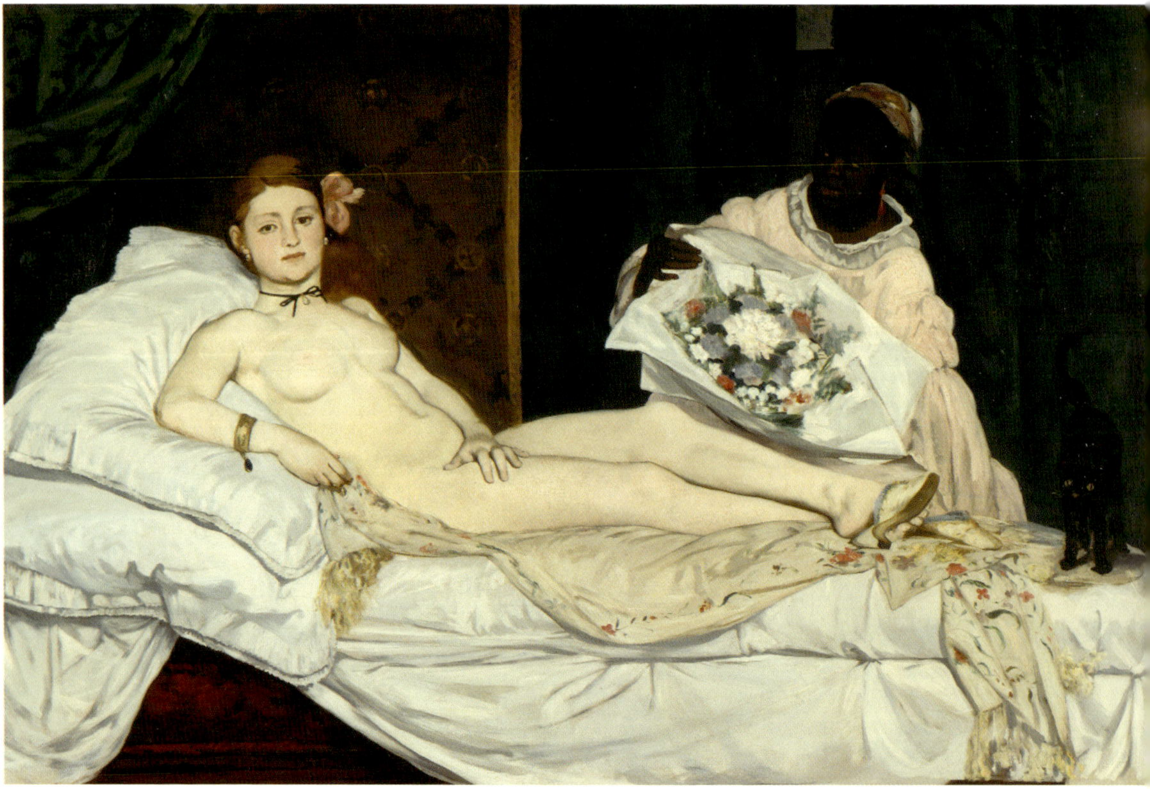

Courtisan: *Socially relatively high ranking woman who seduces her admirers in exchange for certain favours.*

In those days, artists presented their works every year at major exhibition venues called Salons. In the year when **Edouard Manet** paints his "Olympia", **Alexandre Cabanel,** the main official painter shows his "Birth of Venus" at the 1863 salon. What a perfect beauty! *Venus* appears to us as in a dream. Everyone admires her. The emperor Napoleon III acquires the painting. Two years later, Olympia is exhibited in turn. It's a scandal: "Look at her! This is no goddess but a flesh and blood woman!". Manet paves the way for modern painting.

Compare Venus to Olympia. Which of the two women seems more alive, more realistic to you?

Venus: *Goddess of love and Beauty; since Antiquity she represents in Arts the perfect incarnation of physical beauty. It wasn't shocking to represent a nude as long as she was an inaccessible divinity.*

PICNIC

When the empress Eugenia discovers this painting she is outraged. "Good gracious! How indecent: a naked woman standing between two dressed men!". In 1863 at the "Salon des Refusés" **Manet** exhibits Victorine, Olympia's nude model. She is turning around to look at us. What does she think about? Just as in a still life, the picnic basket is spilt over the blue dress.

This painting includes various genres, still life, nude, landscape and portrait. Try to identify them.

Salon des Refusés: Napoléon III opens up rooms for the works rejected by the official jury of the Salon, and leaves it to a curious public to judge for himself.

Soon thereafter, **Claude Monet** paints his version of a "Déjeuner sur l'herbe". Live subjects as tall as nature are picnicking on a lawn. Monet went to the forest of Fontainebleau with Camille, his future bride and his friend Bazille, in order to make a few preparatory studies. He paints the tree leaves in *impasto,* then Monet paints the hudge canvas in his atelier.

Compare Manet's Déjeuner to that of Monet.

Impasto: *Thick layer of painting.*

GARDEN

Thanks to the invention of new painting tubes and pre-prepared canvases, travelling and painting outdoors becomes easier for artists. Whilst traditionally paintings are still made indoors, Monet makes his first entirely open air painting in the garden. Four women dressed in their crinoline skirts day dream in the shadow of a tree or under a sunshade. One of them picks roses in the sun to complete her flower bouquet.

Monet's atelier is his garden! He wants to "catch the light and throw it as it is on the canvas", he says. In spite of the wind, rain, cold and the change of light hampering the work, impressionists prefer to paint their subjects out in the open. They particularly appreciate the daylight which renders colours so gay and changing according to the sun's position. Monet observes lengthily before applying the slightest paint brush on his canvas.

Who painted those flower bouquets? Manet or Monet?

Draw a bouquet indoors and another outdoors.
Do you notice the difference in the light?

Indoors

Outdoors

IMPRESSION

It is 6 am and the sun rises over the harbour of Le Havre in Normandy. From his bedroom **Claude Monet** contemplates the view. "It's magnificent! Quick, my brushes." He has little time. First a general patch of colour, some water, industrial plants, smoke, air. A few lines for the boats against the light and the small waves; a few more for the orange sun light and its reflection in the sea. Here we go: in a few minutes, a sunrise impression!

How long do you think the sun takes to rise?

In 1874, Monet exhibits his painting in the studios of the famous photographer Nadar at the first impressionist artists' exhibition. The exhibiting group of artists was thus christened by an art critic mocking and deeming unfinished Monet's painting title "Impression, soleil levant".

Your turn now, to do an impressionist painting like Claude Monet.

CRADLE

Rockaby baby... Edma, the sister of the artist **Berthe Morisot** is gently rocking her little baby daughter's cradle. She delicately pulls away the frill of the transparent net. What impression of softness radiates from the painting! Do you remember which lullaby your mother used to sing to you?

All is quite in the garden. How pleasant to have a little nap after lunch! **Claude Monet** starts to paint. His son Jean, plays a construction game in the shade. But who left his straw hat in the branches of the tree?

Find the details in the picture.

SWING

What a pretty dress! Jeanne the dressmaker is swinging while chatting. **Auguste Renoir** paints his neighbour. Light is slanting through the tree leaves and forming blue and yellow patches on the ground. Everything seems as buzzing as a swarm of butterflies.

On top of the Butte Montmartre, the *guinguette* is out "on the toot". There is a ball at the "Moulin de la Galette" with orchestra and dancing. Men in top hats or straw hats put their arms around young shop girls and treat them with lemonades. What joie de vivre!

Guinguette: *Venue where people come to relax, often by drinking and dancing outdoors.*

Spot Jeanne at the ball. She's changed gown and hairstyle but is still wearing the same necklace. What is she doing? Can you spot children?

BALLERINA

"Grace and aloofness above all, young ladies…!" The dancing class is started a long time ago. The ballet master is resting on his tall stick and has a ballerina rehearsing her reverence. Without paying any attention to the painter's presence, the other ballerinas in tutus take this opportunity to rest. In the back, mothers attend the rehearsal. On what object is the dancer in yellow tutu sitting?

How lucky! Thanks to **Edgar Degas** we are introduced into the "Foyer de la danse" at the Opéra de Paris. Only a few elected ones have the privilege to catch a glimpse of the ballet's rehearsals between pumps and white poplin tutus. After watching carefully the gracious moves of the ballerinas, Degas retires to his atelier to paint them from memory.

Observe the details and find them in the picture. Can you spot odd numbers?

HAIR

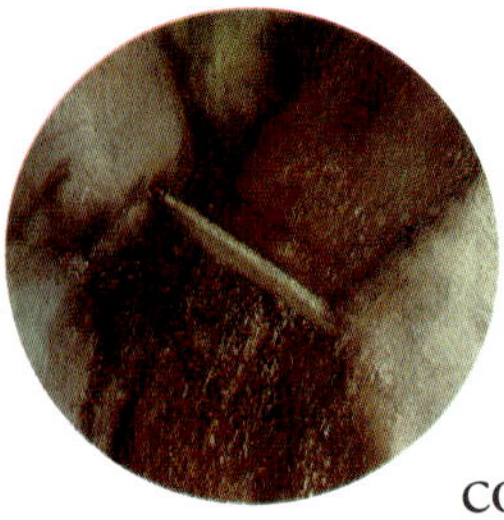

What long hair! A seated lady is untying her endless red hair. Degas likes to paint women in their intimacy. This one seems to be playing a musical instrument. What imaginary instrument could she be playing?

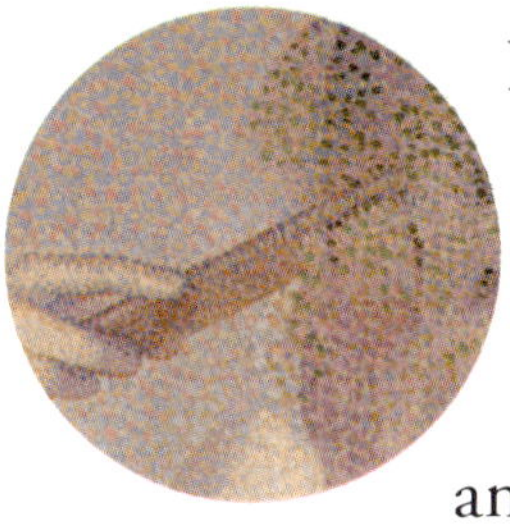

Henri Edmond Cross also painted a woman combing her hair. It is materialized by a collection of small round blue, ocre and green points. The colour division makes the hair flow gently in a mix of light and shadow. They form oscillating waves and hide the woman's face.

Compare the painting by the impressionist Degas to the neo impressionist painting of Cross. Which one is made of pastel colours?

SUNDAY

Finally it's Sunday! What if we went for a walk on the big island of the Grande Jatte? Thanks to the new railway, Parisians, bourgeois and workers, come to relax on the Seine's banks. Women are wearing hats and very tight corsets! Under their skirts: a wicker basket, the very fashionable "cul de Paris".

How many sunshades can you count in the painting?

Aged 25 **Georges Seurat** invents a new technique: divisionism or pointillism. During six months, Seurat sketches open air preparatory studies on the island. Then point by point in his atelier, he assembles 40 characters floating in the landscape. Time seems as if suspended.

Find the details in the picture.

'Cul de Paris'

Bourgeois in top hat

Saint-Cyrien militaries

Trumpeter

Rowing boat

Rower

Embroidery

Nurse

Monkey

CIRCUS

All in the circus ring! At the Fernando circus a clown pulls up the curtain so as to let us see the rider's number. All dressed in yellow she skips on her white horse's back. Hop! An acrobat makes a somersault. Slap! Mr Loyal snaps his whip like a snake while violins continue playing. Hurray! Bravo! On the benches the audience is exulting; some of them sit in the gallery.

In his last painting, **Seurat** only uses yellow, blue, red and white. He structures them in dynamic lines and also paints the frame with an infinite number of little blue spots. Lines are drawn so as to produce an emotional impact, a feeling. Ascending lines and bright colours generate joy, while descending lines and dark colours convey sadness.

Laughter – Inertia – Tears

Find the emotional axis and the details in the painting.

Horse

Acrobat

Gallery

Violin and mirror

Mr Loyal

Clown and whip

BUOY

How good it is to live! The peaceful little fishermen harbour of Saint-Tropez glitters. The soft evening light caresses the colourful facades. The warm hues of the houses are reflected by the sea. A three mast boat is moored among other boats whilst a red buoy floats lulled by the lapping of the sea.

This painting could only be by a friend of Seurat's! **Paul Signac** wishes however to give colours "every possible freshness". He applies on his canvas rectangular touches of wider and purer colour than Seurat's juxtaposed points. Colours come out brighter.

Draw the port of Saint-Tropez in warm and cold tones.

PORTRAIT

By summer night, the scintillating lights form shadows reflected on the ground. A lady takes the air on a terrace lined with rhododendrons and green plants. She holds a closed fan in her hand covered in a glove and turns around to us: "Good evening". Who might she be?

Henri Edmond Cross portrays his future wife in a long black gown. But how should one divide the colour black in a pointillist way? Cross meticulously applies small regular drops of *contrasted colour* on the canvas and patiently alternates between red and blue points…Look at the painting from a distance. Do you see the colour black emerging?

Contrasted colours: *Any colour spreads its complementary colour on its environment; a red object shall for example project green around itself, violet projects yellow, blue projects orange.*

Concentrate 2 minutes on the blue square. Then fix your gaze on the white surface around it. What do you see?

SELF PORTRAIT

What an intense gaze! The Dutch painter **Vincent Van Gogh** spent two years in Paris and met impressionists and neo impressionists. Through their influence Vincent gives up dark colours and lightens up his own palette. His painting brush becomes more daring.

As Van Gogh has very little money, he can't afford a model, so he paints himself. In Paris only, he dashed off 24 *self portraits.* The painter looks at himself in the mirror and ponders. Who am I? Of an anxious nature, he paints with vigorous and tormented paint brushes, through which he can express himself.

Self portrait: *Portrait of an artist by that same artist.*

As Van Gogh, do your self portrait. Look at yourself in the mirror and try to reveal your character.

PARADISE

What bliss! In the summer of 1904, **Henri Matisse** joins his friend Signac in Saint-Tropez. He discovers the latter's painting technique and wonders how "extraordinarily the colour resonates through the use of this technique!". Matisse also decides to embark upon a pointillist adventure.

Matisse rents a modest cottage on the Graniers beach and paints, with bright wide paint brushes, an ideal landscape representing the first day of Creation or is it simply a picnic on the beach under a Mediterranean pine tree. Matisse is inspired by a painting by Cross of 1893, but his colour technique is already quite different.

Compare Matisse's painting to that of Cross.

Text: Catherine de Duve
Graphic designer: Philippe Plumhans
Concept: Kate'Art Editions & Happy Museum!
Translation: Alexa Parr

Photographic credits:

© **Paris, Réunion des musées nationaux**
H. Lewandowski/R.-G. Ojeda
Edouard Manet: *At the beach*, 1873: p.2, *Olympia*, 1863: p.4, p.9, *Le Déjeuner sur l'herbe*, 1863: p.7, p.9 ♣ **Alexandre Cabanel**: *The Birth of Venus*, 1863: p.5 ♣ **Claude Monet**: *Red poppies at Argenteuil*, 1873: cover, p.2, *Sketch of an outdoors subject: Woman under a parasols looking left*, 1886: cover, *Sketch of an outdoors subject: Woman under a parasole looking right*, 1886: cover, *Le Déjeuner sur l'herbe*, 1865-1866: p.7, p.9, *Woman in the garden*, 1867: p.8-9, *Lunch; decorative pannel:* p.13, ♣ **Berthe Morisot**: *Cradle*, 1872: cover, p.12, *Butterfly hunt*, 1874: p.2 ♣ **Pierre-Auguste Renoir**: *Bal at the 'Moulin de la Galette'*, 1876: cover, p.2, p.15, *Swing*, 1876: p.14 ♣ **Edgar Degas**: *The Tube*, 1886: p.2, *Young 14 year old ballerina or Elder dressed up ballerina*, 1879-1881: cover, p.17, *Dance class*, 1874: p.16-17, ♣ **Camille Pissarro**: *Young country woman making fire, white frost, or the burning of fields*, 1887-1888: p.2 ♣ **Georges Seurat**: *Circus*, 1891: cover, p.1, p.22-23, *Subject posing from the back*, 1887: p.2, ♣ **Paul Signac**: *The Red buoy*, 1895: p.3, p.24 © SABAM 2005 ♣ **Henri Edmond Cross**: *The Golden Islands, The Islands of Huyères (Var)*, 1891-1892: p.3, *The Hair*, ca. 1892: p.19, *Mrs Hector France, later Mrs Henri Edmond Cross*, 1893: p.26, *Evening breeze*, 1893-1894: p.31 ♣ **Georges Lemmen**: *Beach at Heist*, 1891: p.3 ♣ **Maximilien Luce**: *The Seine in Herblay*, 1890: p.3 ♣ **Vincent Van Gogh**: *Van Gogh's room in Arles*, 1889: cover, p.3, *Portrait of the artist*, 1889: p.28 ♣ **Henri Matisse**: *Luxury, calm and pleasure*, 1904: p.30 © Succession H. Matisse/SABAM, 2005

© **Bridgeman Art Library/Giraudon**
Georges Seurat: *A Sunday afternoon on the island of la Grande Jatte*, 1884-1886: p.20-21

With special thanks to: Daniel de Duve, Éléonore, Stanislas and Anne-Sophie Sibille, Joséphine and Ferdinand Vanderborght and all those who helped for the making of this book.

Already published: Voici Junior, 2000 • Big Museum!, 2003 • The Secret of Fernand Khnopff, 2004 • Turner Whistler Monet Junior, 2004
Forthcoming: The Little Magritte, 2005 • The Little Klimt, 2005